Rex's Box

By Mary Pat Doyle

Illustrated by Elizabeth Butler

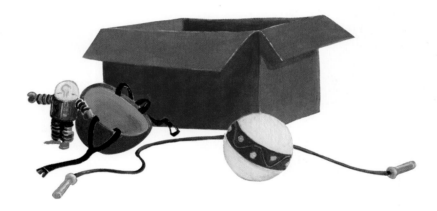

Target Skill Consonant *Xx*/ks/

PEARSON

Scott
Foresman

I am Rex.

I am six.

I have a box.

It is a big red box.

I like my box.

I can look in my box.

I can get in my box.

I can dip and tip in my box.

I rip my box.

Dad can fix my box.